Dedicated to my Dad,
who always encouraged my creativity,
and who I will always miss.

Forever Near

Written and illustrated by Alissa Anderson

Grief may come, it's okay to feel

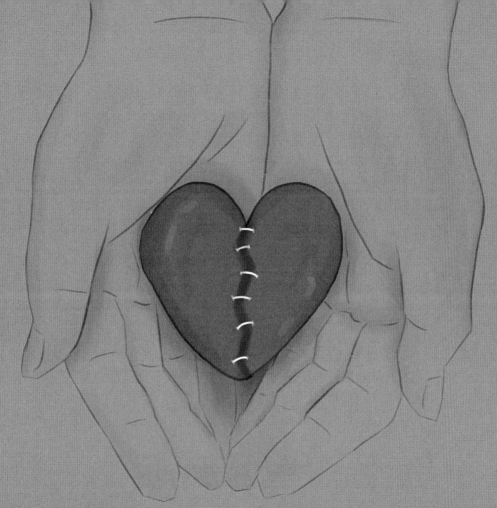

Hearts can hurt, but time can heal.

Tears may flow, like a gentle stream

Hold on tight to each sweet dream.

Memories shine, like stars at night,

Guiding us through the toughest fight.

Love remains, forever near,
even when a loved one isn't here.

In the quiet moments. when we feel low,
remember the love that continues to grow.

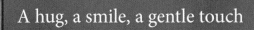

A hug, a smile, a gentle touch

These memories we cherish so much.

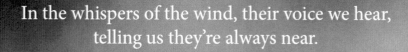

In the whispers of the wind, their voice we hear,
telling us they're always near.

Each day may bring its own sorrow,
but joy will come again tomorrow.

Embrace the sadness, let it be,
for healing takes time, wait and see.

Through the seasons, through the years,
their love in our hearts, forever appears.

In the songs we sing, in the stories we tell

Their presence around us,
we know so well.

Their laughter echoes in our mind,
in the memories we hold, solace we find.

Look up at the sky, at the birds in flight,
know that they watch over us day and night.

Plant a seed, watch it grow,
just like our love, it continues to show.

With each sunrise, with each gentle rain,
their spirit lives on, in joy and in pain.

Reach out to others, share your grief,
in unity and support find relief.

The journey of grief is not alone,
in the love of others, seeds of hope are sown.

Embrace the memories, both big and small,
they are the threads that connect us all.

And when the night feels especially long,
remember their love, forever strong.

In the book of memories, their story's clear,
their love, their light, forever near.

Alissa Anderson was born in Watertown, South Dakota to Don and Traci Anderson, and is the youngest of two children. Alissa moved between South Dakota and Oklahoma for the majority of her childhood, finally settling in Oklahoma in 2018.

Creativity was always encouraged within the Anderson household, which heavily influenced the youngest of the bunch. Alissa is studying at the Minneapolis College of Art and Design to get her bachelors degree in fine arts and is set to graduate in 2028.

Made in the USA
Las Vegas, NV
17 April 2024